In *Water Signs*, Liz Kellebrew reflects o⎯ and the natural and unnatural ways ⎯ ⎯⎯ ⎯⎯⎯⎯. Humorous, illuminating, and unafraid to peel back the complicated layers of living, this collection probes as much as it cradles. Kellebrew asks, "How does one cope with the uncertainty?" Her answers are manifold and, ultimately, hopeful. "Extend that love to yourself: make your heart a homestead."

— Jessica Gigot, author of *Feeding Hour*

Lithe as shoreline madronas, Liz Kellebrew's poems navigate the Salish Sea in reflections on nature, everyday solitude, and a changing environment. Effortless imagery pairs with staunch insights to create a mesmerizing read.

—Gail Folkins, author of *Light in the Trees*

In *Water Signs*, a startling, heartfelt, and brave catalogue of the world around us, Liz Kellebrew echoes Mary Oliver's instructions: "To pay attention, this is our endless and proper work." Whether describing the feral beauty of a post-apocalyptic landscape, taking inventory of her surroundings, or playing with the trope of a midlife crisis, Kellebrew's language is lush and unrelenting, praising the clutter of human life as it intersects with natural world: "The sticky residue on a galley table, spilled juice or sticky bun. Scratched enamel, graffiti of keys," and "Sweetgum seeds cluster in fractals,/ Spiny urchins ambitious as globes." The result is a voice tender as it is stoic, reminding us that there are, "No predators here but us."

— Kendra DeColo, author of *My Dinner with Ron Jeremy*

Water Signs

by

Liz Kellebrew

Variations of "Island Compass," "Salmon Song," and "Puget
Shores" were previously published as parts of "A Music of Ribs"
in Miracle Monocle.

Attention schools and businesses: for discounted copies on large
orders, please contact the publisher directly.

For information contact:
Unsolicited Press
Portland, Oregon
www.unsolicitedpress.com
orders@unsolicitedpress.com
619-354-8005

Cover Design: Kathryn Gerhardt
Editor: Kristen Marckmann

ISBN: 978-1-956692-30-3

Contents

Water Signs

Genesis

If we did start over with
      a new Earth,
Where would we begin?
Would we be wiser and let well enough alone?
Or would our first priority be
Bringing back the iPhone?

Pre:incarnation

I shall write of a time long ago
That is not so different from yesterday,
That is almost the same as tomorrow
But with one difference:
You won't be around to witness it,
Not in your mortal shell.
But maybe you were there, by the riverside,
In the crabgrass under the hoof
Of the draft horse, slender with hunger,
Whose fetlocks were covered with mud.
And maybe you were there, in the shallows,
In the glint of a minnow's eye,
In a buttercup yellow with pollen,
Your heart a bright sun deep inside.

Curvature

How time unfolds,
Like the space between the crests of waves.

Ferry Crossing: Spring

Crossing Elliott Bay:
Mount Rainier due south,
Mount Baker north.
No question which direction you're heading.

So many greens:
True cedar's new bundles of needles,
waxy madrona leaves,
dry scales of western red cedar,
dark greens of hemlock and fir,
the maple's new leaves like opening claws.
Clover and grass shin-high,
clumps of daisies small and godlike,
ever-seeing.

Blue:
The waters of the Sound, bluer than sky,
bluer than blue jeans.
A blue so blue it is black and white,
a blue that is purple in the troughs between waves.

White:
The sky, as is proper.
A haze of mist through which the ferries pass,
steely as guns, buoyant as toys.

Inside:
The sticky residue on a galley table,
spilled juice or sticky bun. Scratched enamel,
graffiti of keys meant for opening
locks, vehicles, homes,
places private and small,
shrunken to the comfort of our animal minds.
No predators here but us.

Hydrophilic Age

They were living in the time of great water,
Trying not to rub their eyes
As the sea level rose and covered the earth.
The trees returned to sea kelp,
Red alder to coral reef,
Lizard legs returned to fish bone,
Horsehair to jellyfish,
Tentacles barbed with lace,
Hoof and antler became web and fin,
Torque and dynamo, fluid wind.
We all became weightless,
We learned how to swim.
Only the birds did not need to change,
And instead grew in span
Like pterodactyls,
Good luck dragons, Pegasus steeds,
And the seed of man was scattered in the ocean depths
Like insignificant krill.

Id

Layer upon layer,
How our darknesses are built.
Light upon light,
Many colors in the shades of
Our fathers' eyes.
The mother's womb lies open to
The ultraviolet light,
Ever reaching, ever pulsing
Divine birthright.

Upon which colors will my flag be flown?
And which heavy flowers laid upon my breast?
Wilting in the desert heat.
A toad, a salamander flickers,
A monarch flutters torn.
No refuge for cryptographers,
The lesson here is none.

If I could choose between the echo of air
Still in a quiet room
And the susurration of synapses
Passing electrons in my unquiet brain,

I would choose neither.
And, in the cool moss fragrance of forest air,

I would lay down my armor
And let myself breathe again.

Equinox

In my heart's eye I know
The earth is tilting toward spring,
Riven inside a strait sea of brilliance,
The robins abluster with reverence.

The Artist's Garden

My love is an act of war,
and my garden is defiance.
In it, I plant seeds of treason:
corn, barley, scarlet beans,
an eyelash, a hangnail, a tooth,
a postcard, a pencil, a page from a holy book.
I cover my seeds with earth and water them in the sun.

Everywhere my fruit grows wild.

Essential Activities

Where do you go when you are already
On the edge of the world,
And the juncos and Steller's jays are *kraw*-ing,
And the sky is so blue it could cut you open,
Filet you like a rainbow trout
Organs glistering under the bare white sun?

Maybe you could beat your powerful falcon wings
And land in a naked walnut with your lover.
Or maybe you could suck the tart pink nectar
from the cherry trees,
Wings fast as Anna's hummingbird,
Skewering your spear tongue down those tiny throats.
Or maybe you could crow-watch from the gutter/harbor/wire
As people waddle by with their
Masks and Clorox and dogs,
Imagine them fileted like fat sardines,
So fearful and
So nutritious.

Hunter

The falcon scans,
Perching on a signal tower,
Towers of firs beneath
         his bold white eye.

Mice in the brush,
Sparrow and thrush,
Scurry, hurry,
         rush.

Summer Grocery Receipt

Single stem flower
Pint strawberries
Large lemon
Red Roma tomato

Spring at the Alehouse

The stripes and ripples of mill-planed wood
Support my pint.
Is it maple? Ash?
Planks of unknown pedigree
Once were felled in an unsilent wood
With a crash so loud,
Everyone heard it.

The maple trees on Winslow Avenue
Uncurl starfish leaves.
Sweetgum seeds cluster in fractals,
Spiny urchins ambitious as globes.

A sandwich board sign for lavender
Is suddenly overcome
With white morning-glory trumpets
And blackberry vines with
New fruit you can smell.

Passenger jet pierces the sky
Like a missile, defanged, grotesque,
Innards full of wetly pulsing human hearts,

Gulping oxygen
Like landed fish.

Responsibility

Spilling forward the water of our dreams,
Falling backward onto soft feather pillows,
The sprouting veins reaching for air everywhere,
Every when.

All at once, in this time which is presence
Of the mind of the body,
Whole-souled and wanting.

The geared teeth of lined notebook paper,
Edges set on sour grapes.

Girl with a peach earring,
The other one lost forever in the blue.

"We need more people like you
In this world."
Who do they need in the other worlds?

Those flat-topped Cascade foothills,
Like molars aged a thousand years.

What did you expect us to do?
We thought it would be like the flu.

You, Too, Are Worthy

It is your deep concern for all living things
     that makes you so miserable.
Extend that love to yourself: make your heart a homestead.

Smith Cove

Old duct works, yellow fuel tank (defunct).
Green fern explodes by cornflower sea.

Ship masts lean like cocktail toothpicks.
A water tower stiff as a taxidermized jellyfish.

Parasailer with a purple and sun-yellow chute.
Sun yellow: this yellow
Is almost white.

Forecasts

hot + humid

What is the heat index of myopia?
Who says they know what they can't see?
Why are people with good imaginations
Labeled dreamers, in the pejorative,
As if the ability to envision other worlds
Was a mark of insanity?

cold + dry

There's a desert in the Yukon,
A treeless slope of golden sand.
You could cross it in a day, but no one bothers.
You can see the whole thing from the side of the road.

Except when it snows. Then,
        you'd never know it's there at all.

hot + dry

Phoenix, Arizona. Another desert.
This one long as the eye can see.
Cacti like telephone poles,
spiny Gumbies, obese tuning forks.
They suck up all the water so there's none left for the lizards.
A roadrunner pants in the shade of a parked car
Behind the auto body shop.
Men in rolled-down coveralls and wifebeaters
drink Jarritos in the shade.
The roadrunner's heart beats fast so it won't fry.

cold + wet

Tears on the deck of a northbound ship.
The weather in Forest Grove, Oregon one Leap Day long ago.
The condensation on a brown glass bottle,
Freed from the cooler,
Dripping on the lawn.

colder + wetter

My natural environment.
Nine months of the year.

A great place for mold to grow, for moss
To colonize the roof.
Brown puddles in the driveway shift
Silver-white. Icicles melt as soon as they form,
Falling with a sound like a glacier calving.

We Are Now Arriving in Seattle

One popcorn kernel under a seat,
And no pigeon to eat it.

Glass-eyed skyscrapers,
Insectoid, compounded,
Missing all six legs.

Forge

The hatchet perches on the lip
Of the pit of fossils,
Spits one iron tooth,
Eats music of a ripe volcano.

The mountains win,
The whales win,
A pod of hot mainframes
Swims down the juicy future.

Sudden love making
Everything a sound.

Midlife Crises

Men in their thirties
Posing on the rails at the stern of the ship:
You're fooling no one.

Methods for delaying madness:
Wear headphones. Chew ice. Do improv.

Land masses drift beneath fingers.
Now: a crack the span of a child's foot.
Later: a canyon the size of a river.

A Strategy for Coping

Don't let the bastards get you down.
Also known as,
Give zero fucks unless it really matters.

How do you know what matters?

You don't learn it from someone else, from a think piece
or the news.
You don't learn it from a podium or a protest.

What really matters is that thing you feel
when you are most alone,
Especially when you're scared.
When you think you're alone with your thoughts,
Only to realize that most of what you thought you knew
was meaningless.
What you know is another person's theory,
someone else's dream.

Or maybe what you know is no one's dream,
Just the artificial intelligence of robot economies,
The circular machinery of plastic echosystems,

The weary grudge of progress.

When you find what really matters, you will know.
It will be unique to you and universal to all,
A golden thread of connection that pulls the whole of
        the world together
So that when you see the mountains devoid of snow
You feel yourself as heat,
And when you see the owlets huddling in their nest
You feel the nip in the air.
When you drink the water you taste the thoughts of fish,
When you walk the woods you smell the bear.
When the wind blows, you hear the *frush* of feathered wings.
You eat the honey, feel the bee sting,
The hot point of her expiring, a needle
Thrust and broken in the quivering cloth of time.

Wait for It

A morning with no rain in it.
Look, a beautiful thing!
A soft, yellow bumble bee,
Searching for blossoms that have not yet opened.

Immortality

To account for is not the same as accounting. Spinning
        reckless thoughts into hungry webs.
The spider's thirst is not quenched until it lays its eggs; then,
        it is dead.
The salmon is the same,
Unless it stays in the ocean forever.
Would it ever die then?

Surface Tension

Stop being so heavy, body.
Look:
If you stretch out,
You can float.

I've been a capitalist since birth.
My parents told me to share,
I screamed No!

The dark shadow in the deep
Might be a current,
Or the boat's reflection,
Or the ghost of a great whale
Still swallowing the sea.

Clearing

There are no empty pages.
Only words that haven't been shared yet.
Only trees, these tall Douglas firs
At the housing development worksite,
Crashing like ships into the bedrock of earth.
A small man with a chainsaw, buzzing.
Seven-thirty in the morning.
The Himalayan blackberry vines return with thorns that slice
       the flesh.
Calves sting in the shower, pink water down the drain,
Draining to the Sound, feeding dogfish and octopi.
Anemones flower and spasm. Barnacles defy gravity.
Cormorants flare and stoop,
   dive,
   rise,
take to the air.

Permamelt

Smoking handrails orbit
The cumulus nematode.
A sunstroke of polar bears
Migrates down the Coast Guard
Oil wells up from radio towers
Drenching the airwaves with heat.

Heave

Pluck me a cherry blossom pier
Piped clean on the washboards of frogs.
Sudden wax dusting gold pans,
Bedpans portal to seraphic spheres.
The mother digits, bored to life,
Eke Pleaides from bread bags,
Tie parabola flights into turkey necks,
Eat clock hand wattles by the pound.

Primordial Compost

A paper tub of ketchup and relish rests on the windowsill.
The things we throw away—tomatoes, cucumbers, trees.
We are the only species that actively destroys
        the things that sustain us.

Meanwhile, the universe conspires to keep us alive.
Just look at the oceans in our blood,
the trees in our lungs,
the starstones deep in our bones.

Summer, Eagle Harbor

Brown smoke holds low the mountains.
Seagulls scream.
The trees are gold with harvest.
The humble houseboat dreams.

Suspicious Activity

Strategies for exiting an airborne aircraft:
> Don't.
> Put on a parachute.
> Sprout pterodactyl wings.
> In case of a water landing, know how to swim.

On ships, fullness thereof:
> Get comfortable.

On people who see what's not there:
> If you see something,
> (please, for the love of God) don't say something.

Thoreau as a Post-postmodern Woman

On wild apples: so many, so much
They roll into the gutter like a thousand
Bowling balls, no pins in sight.

On hangnails, pain thereof:
Don't grit your teeth.
Pare back the wild flesh and wrap your finger in a bandage,
As if your own body did not gift to you this wound.

On wearing all white:
I'd only be confident if all I ate was Wonder bread,
And I had my tubes tied.

On comfort:
It exists only in your mind.

Fog: the cloak of indifference,
The shadow of clouds,
The clarity when heaven falls to earth.

Defiance: climbing the radio tower
And painting your name there

Over and over and over again.

The question, do I know you? becomes,
Should I know you? Do you know me?
Must I know you?

Finn's First Ecstasy

The apple fell from the tree.
This was its first act of independence.
It followed, naturally, that I should sink my teeth
into its speckled flesh, but
not until I touched its red-yellow-green skin with my own,
a poke of finger, grip of palm,
saw the one brown puckered crater
where a worm emerged or burrowed,
flight or home, nest or astronaut, I knew not, and
not until I plucked the ragged green leaf
from its wooden stem,
inhaled the sweet rot scent of the fallen apple's ferment
did I sink my teeth into its speckled red-yellow-green flesh and
taste the burst of wet fruit salivation,
exulting flowers in the thrust of bees' tongues,
grainy pulp a testament to the endurance of my flesh.
Expense only the apple's own, and whose fault is that?
We eat the things with lifespans shorter than ours,
we pluck and winnow, reap and bone,
trap, rake, spear, scythe.

Gideon Park

Blue periwinkles, one fat bumble bee,
Wind in my face walking south and east.
Sunlit green grass and red-brown fir cones,
A child's tennis shoes, abandoned at play.
Azaleas erupting in living flower,
A royal carpet leading to the woods.
The corvids nesting and flustered,
Clear sap trail down the pine tree's trunk.
If you lick it, you will taste the sweet.

Downhome

Under a clear blue day,
Sky glass water hollow
Nets snag the bones of fishes.
Pressed grapes burn the father tongues.
Gas spills on the children.
The match is lit,
Spurring the axe head on.

Unpaid Overtime

What is labor? Is it something you do for money?
Is it an activity that makes you sweat?
Is it something that requires skill, or is it a rote task?
Is it something that you're proud of?

If making things is what sets us apart from the animals,
Is labor how we set ourselves apart from other people?

The Ophthalmologist Asks If I'm from Arizona

No, I was that kid who stared too long at the sun,
Always walking around in zigzag, cornmeal circles
With plasma burns on my retinae.
Pink spots, black blobs, blue, white, green
Streaks of cloudshine ray-ning on my occipital lobes
Like chunk saw lasers,
Like the neon musk lights at the roller rink,
A rumble of hornets disturbed in terry cloth short shorts,
A head full of clown red hair,
Candy floss furry as weeks-old mold,
A toothache for a lifetime.

The Problem with Stories

Tools: knives, nutcrackers, rakes
Weapons: grenades, potatoes, ice skates

One of these things is not like the others.
One of these things just doesn't belong
                                    . . . but why?

Why apples vs. oranges, and not just fruit?
Why do word problems have numbers?
And why does data require user stories?
What angle is more acute than the pain of not belonging?
What difference is not a problem to be solved?

Resisting someone else's category makes you unusable
In their word problem user story.

The problem with stories is the uncategorizable word.

Apokalypsis: an unveiling, a revelation

When the golden trumpet falls
And the earth shatters open,
The new chasms gush forth rivers.
You can hear the early robins
Calling dibs on earthworms after the rain,
After the hail has piled under the pines
On High School Road like snowdrifts.

Venus suns her way into the party of Pleaides,
Sisters reunite every eighth year
In the house of pure love.
We breathe in, exhale,
Release the fear,
Become boneless with peace.

Finn in the Rain

When he walked behind the waterfall, Finn felt safe.
It was the same feeling beneath the rainy sky—
His skin cold and washed clean,
Safe from the glaring eyeball of the sun,
Whose holiness was too gold to spare anyone,
Least of all Finn.

The salmon rejoiced in the downpour—
Their streams overflowed.
The mighty fish muscled their way
Through the rushing waters,
Great toothed jaws gasping as if for breath,
As if the air was too much for them,
A weight greater than water.

Annual Maintenance

What is the function of a ship?
Its tangent the sum of its rust-covered hull,
Divided by cosines of water.
The weight of so many barnacles
Pulling it down like a millstone,
Growing heavier,
Familiar over the years.

Scrape that off,
You don't need it.

September, Madison Avenue

On a morning with nothing but rain,
Reds seem redder.
The last of the summer daisies
Display themselves against gray cedar fences,
The dead and dying flowers bow down like penitents.
Yellow raincoats emerge,
Cars and trucks move slower,
Slosh more, honk less.
Umbrellas defy gravity.

Unsheltered

Look at you, beautiful day,
With eyes wide and skin so blue,
Your cloudlings relentless as ships,
Your birch bridge between earth and sky
As forked and branching as time.
You make my heart go BOOM.

Undertow

This is how the river broke my heart:
It made promises it couldn't keep,
Talking all night while I tried to sleep.
Relentless, exhausting, it churned,
Eroded the banks, rushed over salmon,
Brought eulachon and trout,
Exhilaration and doubt.

The river runs like mad, like madness,
In waves and currents stern and
Gentle, piercing,
A slick stab wound on the face of the earth.

Dry Docked

The ferry ships park in the harbor,
Deck lights on,
Windows dark,
The trees on Hall's Hill darker still.

A ship is a circle,
A forest, a labyrinth,
A fence, a series of squares imposed on the sky.
Who dares to box the sky?

We need a space wall
Built by Space Force,
So we can fight our wars in the exosphere,
Protecting Earth with a layer of rocket fumes and
        spent bombs.

(But if nothing explodes in space, what's the point?)

Changelings

In the future, we shall all be changed
into ogres or sprites or
something more gelatinous—
jellyfish, amoebas, sweet crude oil.

No animals will disturb our flesh
(except for maybe the carnivores),
and even they will only eat us
as a last resort.

Yellow

Hazard paint, beachfront homes,
Autumn leaves,
Raincoats, my Timberland boots,
A wedding ring,
Hair,
Sports cars,
Bumble bees,
Mustard,
The Winchell's Donuts logo,
Sulfur, urine, jaundice,
Reflective vests,
Crime scene tape,
A category in Pictionary,
Cheese fondue

Ferry Crossing: Fall

Crossings between cities,
Crossing over
The spirits of the sea between.

Flannel working on laptop, smartphone on windowsill,
Desperate for a signal.

Three old men discuss architecture and Wichita,
One's wife speaks of carnations.

Pineapple shirt paces on deck.
Two friends speak intently with their hands.
Tourists in baggy jeans
Capture photos and tater tots.

Trenchcoat, polished shoes
Falls asleep next to me.
Behind me, long nails on computer keys, clacking.

Fluorescent yellow raincoat
Burns a hole in the slate gray sky.
A professional camera wanders,

Framing skyscrapers.

One-dimensional

Coastlines aren't really lines at all.

Social Tediums

A good meal and a good fuck
Followed by a good night's sleep—
The cure for what ails most folk under 40.

A passing smile, a brief stare,
A side-eye of sly admiration.
The safety of knowing
That shit will never go anywhere,

Not like the other shit
That seeps from the news,
Drips from media platforms like an oil of viruses
Sticking to every surface and
Crawling on the water.

I walk hard on the fistfight
That is the spine
of
the island.

Islands roll, they don't walk.
They don't say much, but they'll give you a look,

A look that says what they really think about you.

Island Compass

I have been still in the south,
where the island meets the water,
madrona and fir trees kissing the sea.

I have been still on the cliff where the Nootka roses grow,
where Anna's hummingbird hides among the blackberries.

I have been still in the west, in the lap of the ocean,
her waves warm and cold washing over me.

I have witnessed the passing of whales and sea lions,
their bodies left behind to feed those who come after.

I have been still in the east,
where the last stars meet the first star,
Venus shining like a precious stone.

I have sat among the lilacs with a plywood guitar,
singing songs to the morning with joy in my heart.

I have been still in the north, where the dancers by the fire
dance the night of ancient days.

And high upon the mountain I have seen a red fox,
and we were not afraid.

Salmon Song

What is the wavelength of a soul?
From trough to crest the height and crest to crest the length.
Lifted by the wind, the moon,
the fragile spirits of fish bones floating on the surface.

There was a hunger for food in the deeps,
a hunger for plankton and midges and fry.
I was hungry to explore,
to go where my mother and father had gone before me,
to plumb the great salt secrets of the sea.

They do not tell you of the hunger to go home.
This hunger does not come when you are young.
That is not what it is for.

Cut me open. See the rings in my flesh.
Count the years of my being in the palm of your hand.
My body is like ripples on a pond.

The wind blows from the west,
sighing for the east,
water dreaming of sky.

Collected

Today, I will write about the things
I do *not* know:
Stellar clouds, dung beetles, yellow cake,
Principalities and powers,
Subterranean bunkers,
Religious wars and holy undies,
Undead pets, durian fruit, blue roses,
The way the ground rumbles beneath the treads of a
            military tank,
The taste of held breath in the seconds before the bomb,
How the bridge feels when you jump off,
Heart yanked to your feet
By the bungee cord.

Wagenstraat

The thing about canals is
They don't tell you
About the mosquitoes
The size of gondolas,

Nor the men who spit
When you walk
Over the bridge,
Toxic as malaria.

Madronas

Redder than the redwoods,
Slender, graceful, buoyant,
Tall as turrets,
Powerful as castles,
Flexible as dancers.
Stronger than the wind,
They bend,
They sometimes break,
But the trunk is strong
When roots run deep.

Plasticity

What does it mean to think elastic?
Do androids dream of elastic sheep?
Does time itself stretch? Hot taffy
Between recalcitrant fingers,
Butter pooling cold.

Have you considered the cost vs. benefits
Of a cattle prod?
Efficient, potentially deadly.
Can be used against its owner.
Rewires neurons.
Costs a measly hundred smackers.

Under a gray-blue sky at morning,
The trees smolder electric green.

Exchange

Windows, doorways, tunnels the same,
Permit entrance to
Light, fragrance, sound.
Ocarinas deep under the ziggurat,
Fresh baked waffle cones wafting
Down the sidewalk.
Rain, clouds, sun, and moonlight
Entice the senses.
Come, travel between worlds,
Leave yours for mine.

Register

The hot-pitched hum the ferry makes
As it moves into the wind,
A slight odor of sulfur,
A column of steam rises across the Sound.
Fog clouds lift.
The League of Women Voters will
Sign you up to vote
Across from the galley and the
Urns of burnt coffee.

Citizens United

Imagine it now, if
Neophilia is love of the new,
What's wrong with all the people who love old things?
Antique collectors, museum docents,
Library science majors with minors in
Ancient Sumerian,
Muscle car fanatics, cinephiles,
Practitioners of martial arts and
Religions older than Christ,
Who, by the way, appeared at
A Seattle City Council meeting
On behalf of a Green New Deal
And the people cheered.
Now Jesus is a Muslim and a Jew,
And his followers are all confused
Because no one told them that loving the old ways
Doesn't mean they can't love the new.

Double negatives can't be trusted and
Neither can CEOs of anything,
Except maybe tax software companies
And non-profit animal shelters,

Which don't have CEOs anyway.

If a corporation is a person,
How does it identify?
Pan, trans, cis, het, Asian, straight?
Gay, Black, white, Native, Latinx, big-boned, overweight?
Anorexic supermodel, hot dog eating contest winner,
Eating everything we make and spewing it back up?
Collecting billions of American dollars
And not paying taxes on the software
Or the planes or trucks that bring
Warehouses to the people
Who all think their banana slicers
Come from the cloud.

It's a Trick

The cake is a lie.

Every human for humanity.

The robots win.

Alternate History

Well, this is an auspicious start.
A fortuitous retelling
Of the story of the American West,
Which never really belonged to
Amerigo Vespucci after all
(He never set foot here).
And, also, just because people put their feet
On a patch of dirt doesn't make it theirs.
Does it?

Progress

She ran a tight ship.
You can change it if you want to,
Copy that,
The mark of the devil, 666.

You could change, but why would you want to?
Change is danger, is evil, is non-compliant.
You might hurt someone or
You might grow,
Like a tree or a fungus,
A fruiting body sprouting from decay underground,
The finned caps peed on by dogs,
Spores scattered everywhere.

It is absolutely worth saving,
Whatever there is left.

Afterlife

A tree that has fallen
Becomes a log,
Becomes a bed of moss,
A nursery,
A mushroom farm,
A beetle's home,
A fox's lair.

The New Normal

Desperate house lives
Inside of ticky-tacky boxes.
Sky high rents and dirt-cheap doors.
Pre-hung windows meet paper-thin walls.
When it's cold out, I don't know you.
When it's hot, we sweat like dogs,
Through our mouths
And the soles of our feet,
Panting so hard we're unable to drink.

The glory of a mountain is its winter.
Snow aglow in the southern sun,
Glaciers that slowly refreeze
Only to burst again next alpine spring,
Flooding the roads and
Everything on them.

Delicate

The undoing is naught to be undone.
There are more wolves here
Than are dreamt of in your limp theosophy.
I am an aristocrat of sound:
Together, we play new melodies,
Only audible in the dense moist air
Of distant planets.
Nearer stars are conquered by desire,
By the wants of fire ants
Swarming their queen.
Monarchy is all but assured. They didn't survive
A hundred generations to crumble
At the first touch of guilt.
They've been weaving there, spawning each birth.
The long wings of corvids, a fang claw waiting.
A finding of rain gutter crumbs.

Automation

Did the world change, or
Did we?
Spools of cable rolling up and down
The arm of the metal crane,
Like bracelets on a Hindu wedding day.
Silks layered on towers like limbs.
Steel, glass, concrete, rebar,
The bodies of the unknowable future.

Meanwhile, a man in a cockpit keeps
Pulling our levers, turning our dials.

Midtown 21

When escalators seize, who removes the offending object?
Shoes, watches, cell phones, pens,
Limbs, wet leaves, small dogs, and children.
Those giant purses women carry, big enough
To hold three men's heads.
Dropped guns, curry lunches, fistfuls of hair,
Wigs, and evening gowns.
Stilettoes and the eyes poked out by them,
Those expensive electronic key fobs,
Pocket calculators, Alexa eyeglasses,
Wax-lined paper coffee cups and
Those plastic ones with sippy cup lids,
De-icing salt that'll rust your gears,
Conveyor belts frayed with time,
And bored mice gnawing at night
When the escalator's turned off.

Feminine

I got my period at the Bremerton WinCo
On aisle 12 by the trays of raw beef.
Eyes like spores exploding all around me,
The hot motherboard smell,
A metal you could taste.
I dodged asteroid swarms of shopping carts,
Sunday's children seizing like bees,
Diabetic porch moms hoarding fruit snacks and cheese,
Navy wives biting cellular coins.
The line for a stall, unmoving.
Restroom floor unmopped for weeks.
Red lava of blood in the water, rising
Like an Easter dawn.

Rain Experts

Basically, she just puts on a slip dress
And a sweater or something. Yeah.

The heron caught a fish today.
He was so still and patient until
It was time to strike,
Then he moved like a snake, ess-necked,
Spear-beaked.

I had these cute little short black boots
That look really cute with this,
But I just didn't want to carry them.

Carrying is hard for something as natural
As greed,
As sharing,
As hoarding all the things we'll never need.

Hey, are you in my office right now?
Well, when you get to my office will you call me from there?

The boots with good tread squeak on the linoleum
when it has rained,

Separating the rain experts
From the rain amateurs.

Plumage

A Denver idea of what's cool:
Faux wool-lined corduroy jackets and herringbone,
That concert hoodie I just bought
With all the dates and places of the tour
I've never been to,
Puffy arctic shells, winter coats to make you sweat,
Yogurt in a plastic bowl from home,
A red pen and a notebook, college lined,
Gulls and marsh birds picking purple sand dollars,
A cookbook, a crampon, and
Those canvas shoes they call boaters,
Worn on an actual boat
(This is either double irony or intent).

Outside, cormorants on the buoys
Flex their wings like wrestling stars.

Finn on the Shore

When Finn stood on the shore,
It seemed to him that the water rolled on forever.
Although he knew there was land on the other side,
Three days by boat and no more,
He let himself believe that his land was the only land,
His people the only people.
He felt both comforted and frightened at this thought.
On the one hand, if it was only them alone,
The world was knowable:
It had observable rhythms, and resources they could gather.
Predictable seasons, and familiar animals, fish, and plants.
Sustenance, shelter, and kinship were all assured.
His people practiced traditions that were older than the eldest
Clansman's ancestors.
The world was safe and sane,
As long as one followed the rules,
And the rules were easy to follow
Because Finn had known them all his life.

But on the other hand, if it was only his people
And no one else,
The world was devoid of inspiration and meaning.

There was nothing to be discovered,
Nothing to be seen for the first time.

No other lands or peoples even a year and a day
by boat from here.
All the creatures and trees were the same everywhere.
It wouldn't matter where he went:
Every place would reek of familiarity,
The way the odor of a home fire clings to your garments
But you are no longer able to smell it.
It was the death of curiosity, of invention, of knowing.
And if there was one standard by which Finn lived his life,
It was knowing.
Knowing meant seeing and hearing. Touching and tasting.
Smelling and understanding that the wind would bring rain.

It might not be the safest life, but it was the one he had.
He pushed his coracle into the water,
Into waves as gray as the sky.
He got in and rowed away.

Navigating

They set out due east from the harbor
And slightly north
To avoid the slumbering kraken.

Vessel #2 Tacoma Delayed by 20 Minutes

We have become unmoored from the dock in Eagle Harbor,
About to cross the wide gray bay.
What's a bottom line, and what's so basic about it after all?
Not much that I can tell.
Hello and hell no
Sound a lot alike.
There are fatigues and then there are spaces.
There are gulls and yellow trees, yellow as yield signs.
The waves are a she/he/they today, all genders in one,
Potential and energy, whitecap and trough.
Sulfur, creosote, diesel exhaust
Just a few of the things that have entered my body.
Coffee and its attendant chemicals,
Plus the microfraction of animal poop allowed by the FDA,
Some insect legs, and a treaty.
I can only imagine how crowded it is
On the passenger deck.
The phone calls, the luggage,
Women and children coping with change feet first,
Like they always must.

Reception

Apple shampoo,
Diet Coke,
A Wi-Fi hotspot held together with electrical tape,
The beep of devices obeying
Like good children and
Good dogs.
Seagull riding the updrafts,
Wings bent,
The original ailerons.
A first look at the whitecaps
Indicates shore erosion.
Orcas feed, the seagull dives,
The women gossip in voices
That are almost whispers
But not quite.
They know the secret art of getting strangers to listen.

For Your Security, Please Stay with Your Luggage at All Times

Coast Guard boat
So tiny you could squeeze it between your fingers,
Pop it like a grape.

Those of us who are not sure,
Let us console you with images of certainty:
A locked door,
A machine gun on a helicopter and a boat,
A sign with a law and a penalty on it,
A flu vaccine,
A chicken's egg,
Incubating sameness,
An untuned piano flat with fear,
The rings on a paper coaster,
The tacky floor of a pub,
The unreality of the real.
A federal cop with arms like breadsticks,
Fat, white,
Easily broken,
Weapons on hips, including zip ties.
To secure who, exactly?

Endurance

Things my ancestors saw are still here:
      Cedar trees, salmon, rivers, apples,
      Racism, poverty, war, fear.

The Right to Dissemble

Churches and shopping malls:
They all have fountains.
Fonts for baptizing and sanitizing or drinking from,
Surrounded by fake green houseplants
In the nave or atrium, where you pause to
Make yourself holy before you enter the sanctuary
That is separated into pews with books and
A medieval banquet of felt
Quilted banners in many colors, not so different from
The repetitive boxy storefronts offering
Several variations on the same merchandise
And hanging advertisements depicting
The descendants of apes
Enjoying chocolate, bras, and soap.
Also, there is music involved:
Something soft and soothing,
Angelic choirs of elevator music.
And there is something akin to preaching:
A sales pitch, a cosmetics rep
Naming the season of your face.
There is food:
Take, eat. My blood, my body,

Coke and pretzel, nacho cheese.
Additionally, one is expected to pay
One-tenth of one's salary
In exchange for eternal salvation or
Aromatherapy mood enhancers,
But either way you still feel empty.
Lastly:
Other people go there too and
You're supposed to feel some sort of kinship or
Social bond,
But really
You're all secretly competing.

Effortless

The trees were all the colors of the rainbow,
Except for blue.
But those are my eyes: blue beholds.
And I ate a piece of warm frybread,
Drank coffee, cracked jokes, smiled,
Made friends, made a phone call,
Ate a healthy lunch, and texted
My honey so they knew I was thinking
Of them.
And the ships were full of orphans
And spray cleaner.
And the grocery store was a maze of carts
And eggs.
And, for all my effort,
I've made no art today.
   Or have I?

Winning

She gives him a long look
That he refuses to return
Because she knows that he knows
    She is right,
And he knows that she knows
    She is right.
And so, an entire evening passes
With three rounds of drinks
And zero conversation.

Westchester

These bare-naked yards,
Where St. Francis lurks like some
Peeping Tom midget ghost
Softly glowing in the dark,
Holding a basin of holy water strategically
Over his junk,
His long robe completely covering his (supposedly) bare feet,
Suggesting both nakedness and sexlessness.
And in the fog, you'll think he's a gangbanger
From the wrong side of the tracks,
Loitering by the window looking to case the joint
And steal your TV and turn on Alexa
While you're visiting the grandkids in Chicago.

Human Hair

Close-shaved, too tame,
Might as well be a helmet.
Just take it off when you park your bike in the garage,
Hang it in the foyer
When you come home from work,
Polish it with Simple Green and Turtle Wax,
Wear it through the car wash.
Tapered, swirled, whorled out
From that one off-center sunburst.
A chin strap is frowned upon but
Might be tolerated in certain circles.
The smell of day-old coffee
And pit-stained button-ups.
The suit and tie, status symbols
For desperation
Or a job at J.C. Penney, which is really the same thing.

Transplant

Here is like everywhere else
But with the privilege of excess water.
How many steps in 0.6 miles?
How much oxygen inhaled?
The world is mine and everything in it
Enters me also.
I too am a vital organ in the ecosystem,
But I can easily be replaced.

Evening Meal, Deep Autumn

I am thankful here,
now,
with your body next to mine,
hot steak and cool water,
red autumn leaves seen through glass,
and the sunset in the sky.
The warm wood of the table,
yellow light of the lamp,
salt and sweet on my tongue,
the rough skin of your knuckles
in the palm of my hand,
gray eyes that might be green
catch fire here,
now.
I am so thankful.

Dwelling Places

Library books,
Red rugs,
Craftsman homes,
Yellow kitchens,
Warm cat or calm fish (or both),
Art on the walls,
A feather duster,
Roast in the pot,
The click of gas burner igniting,
Tea kettle whistle,
Faded linoleum,
Creaky back doors,
Herb gardens and lilac trees,
Scrubbing ink out of the dryer
Because I forgot that a pen is always in my pocket,
Wood floors,
Claw-footed bathtubs,
A painting studio, room to write,
A plaid shirt with long sleeves,
A cup of something hot to drink,
Music, flowers, laughter,
Windows that let in the light,

Cosmic backyard stargazing,
Moons that light up the night.

Waterfront Property

A home built on a sea cliff
Facing southeast, which is really
Smart when you think about it,
Except for tsunami scenarios,
But no one can really be smart with tsunamis.

Survival skills are a lost art,
Like science, or common sense,
Or dressing oneself appropriately
For the weather.

Pampas grass,
The name implies Patagonia,
High prairies, and cold stars,
But, in reality, it's just a transplant
Forced to eke out a living in some gringo's backyard.

If I had a jaguar,
I'd feed it lots of beef
And take it on long walks in the woods.
Perhaps it would bring me some venison.

Crossing Elliott Bay sometimes
Looks like a diorama,

The foothills and mountains layered into the distance
Like cardboard cutouts.

What was Mt. Baker's original name?
(These fall cedars, though—)
Which bird is that? Which tree?
The human desire to name everything.

Sensory

Shameless city,
Gray as a winter's day,
Stark and strong as bone
But just as breakable.

In the distance,
You can see the rain pour down
As if someone were carding
The wool of the clouds.

The roll of luggage wheels overhead,
A sound like thunder.

The water treatment plant in Magnolia,
From here the size of a pencil's tip,
Overflowing nearly as much sewage
As the Navy ships when they dock in Bremerton.

I smell something like blueberry pancakes.
My mouth waters,
Conspiring.

Instincts

Today, I am Bear,
All fur and smoke,
Cold grease from yesterday's meal
Scenting my beard.
I roll up from the ashes of last night's fire.
My eyes made small by the too-bright sun,
I roar.

Today, I am Fish,
Cold and wriggling out from under the covers,
Mouth searching for water and food,
My only desires.
All other human demands wash off me,
Irrelevant.

I am Wolf tonight,
Part canine, part terror.
Friendly enough until
You get too close to my teeth.

Probabilities

When anything is possible,
How does one cope with the uncertainty?
Perhaps there is a trick to it,
This open book called living,
That takes everything into and out of itself
Like a pair of fluttering lungs.

Acceleration

The curved trail of the boat's wake is almost the same
As a path through the woods.
We're out of the harbor now picking up speed.
Two men discuss their children's Halloween costumes,
Laughter ensues.
A ferry worker in a clown mask
Poses for a passenger's selfie.
It is possibly one of the scariest things
I have ever seen.

Life Preservers

Reading quietly: phones, newspapers, a book, magazines,
The New Yorker
All the way out here in Puget Sound.

Knitting green yarn, listening to music.

Coffee, water, the aftermath of fruit—
specifically, a banana peel.

People sleeping, people sneezing.

The hand dryer in the ladies' room
A constant buzz.

Superposition

Upon exiting the ferry,
S/he forgot their phone/wallet/charger/keys/
      bike/car/that they were drunk,
And then came the consequence.

Unpredictable.
Does that even apply to anything?
Or does it merely indicate
That not enough studies have been done yet?

I have studied the heck out of the man I love,
But occasionally he still surprises me.

Anger = an indication that something needs to change.
Madness = somehow, not a synonym for anger.
Synonym = what you say when you want to be different.
Different = 1. [*common*] A problem to be solved.
      2. [*rare*] An inspiration.

View through a Ferry Window

Mirrored rectangles of incandescent light
Stretch out the window and over the waves
Beneath them, a second row of windows
And people reading, nodding, walking
On water.

Shelter in Place

When the tide comes in,
You may as well forget about
Piano keys or
Dyeing your hair or
Ever going back.
You're going to be doggy-paddling in the seaweed
Forever and a day,
Inhaling that rich green algae and
The salty piss of the oyster beds
In the bone-cold water.
Why bones are cold, I don't know,
Because marrow is hot, Hot, HOT.
One little *cordon sanitaire* and
The mind jumps instantly to cannibalism.
Why not, that's only the logical conclusion.

NIMBY

How the new construction plywood
Pops out among the gray established homes
Like a pimple.

Safeway Run

Apocalypse is now, Karen.
No one cares about your reusable bags,
Or why we're all standing here together
At the smart-locked doors of the grocery store
At 5:53 in the morning,
Masked, gloved, and caffeinated,
Admiring the potted boysenberry starts.
We're all mad at that teenage girl in the sweatpants
Who cut off the first four people in line
And grabbed the first of twelve packs of toilet paper
That were sold out in ten minutes' time.
"It's a miracle," someone said.
"Hallelujah," I (sarcastically) said,
But the relief that flooded my body
At the soft thud of tissue in my cart
Was unmistakable as sex.

Commuters

What's it like to wake up every morning
Out of doors
And not by choice?
It's cold out.
You sit up in your sleeping bag.
You're wearing a red sweater,
There at the picnic table by the museum.
You make eye contact with the people walking by.
They're walking dogs, wearing backpacks,
Carrying coffee. They don't have time to stop.
They're all on their way to somewhere,
Somewhere else, a world where people
Spend their days in a boardroom
And their nights in a bedroom,
A world where you don't belong.

Port of Seattle

New terminals, new ports.
Endpoints and beginning points.
Points at the tip of a pencil, or
A fine point pen.
Bullet points,

- BANG
- BANG
- BANG

In a PowerPoint presentation.
In case you didn't get the point,
Here look,
I've already made my point.
The point is that there is no point
In pointing fingers,
Or toes,
Or tongues.
Not to put too fine a point on it,
But you can't be a ballerina
Without pointe slippers.
The ship stutters wordlessly static,
Sliding through the Sound without a sound,
Its many white lights like

The harshly lit mirrors
In a subway restroom.

Meanwhile, on the barge,
Is that grain? Sawdust?
Wood chips? Cornmeal?
What are those unladen piles of gold?

Ferry Chasers

Small boats cross the harbor
Diagonally behind the vee of the larger ship,
Riding the wake.
Those seagulls the size of young eagles
Hunt the silver fish
That roll up in multitudes.

Knots

Dog on a rope,
Yellow rope leash.
A yellow rope like the kind my stepfather used
To tie coolers to the top of the station wagon.
Rear-facing seats in the back,
Brown metallic paint,
The "it" shade at some point in 1970s automobile history,
As if the color of shit with sparkles in it
Were the coolest thing ever.
Who let these Detroit CEOs make decisions anyway?
Look at them now,
The mighty made low,
The mountains flattened
And the valleys pulled straight,
Straight as the doily
On my grandmother's table,
A matter of feminine pride.

Puget Shores

I need not write of the space between wild and tame,
for you already know.
The full moon
on an ice-dry winter night,
the crack of twig and bramble,
thorn and hip of wild rose.
A storm cloud of breath and dark sky twinkling.

The stars are always there.
I see the bright ones in the daytime, white in the blue,
like snowberries dropped by gulls in a peaceful ocean.

M/V Puyallup

When it's too hot in the galley,
You go up on the sun deck.
Except on the sun deck
There isn't much sun right now,
But it's cool with a breeze,
And dogs can roam up here,
And people talk and meditate and read.
They walk into the wind and
Back out of it again.
They eat and sleep and write poems,
Look out over the dark bay
And see the amber city lights,
The lights of other ships crossing
       parallel
       lives.
Living hot in the galley,
In the engine room,
Pulsing in the oil pumps
And fuel lines,
Sparking in ignitions
And rotating calipers,
Gearshafts and drivelines

Syncing with propellers,
Pushing the ship,
Pulling the water through and under.
And up top on the cold wet sun deck,
The wind whistles like wild panpipes,
Fluorescent lights cast fuzzy shadows,
Plexiglass shields you from the night.

Flight Path

Walking in the woods at Fort Ward yesterday
We overheard the Morse code
Of a woodpecker.
Was it pileated?

A bald eagle flew over us also,
Distinguished as Sean Connery.

The southeast is brown this morning
With a hint of gold.
It is the second day
Of meteorological winter.

A Wavelength Meditation

Near the time of winter solstice,
When the sun is still slowly setting
And the clouds are this gray,
Every light is like a miniature sun.
The city is the stars, is the galaxy.
The sky is the dark, is the coming night, the deep unknown.
The black hole at the center of the Milky Way
Is a force, a matter so heavy we cannot see it,
Except for its bursting halo of light.

X

Toad sits still
On the ridge of the nebula,
Tastes the lack of air,
The lack of flies.
Somewhere in the Orion arm
A man is frying Spam,
His sweater smelling of last night's chili.

That's a good solar system,
Toad thinks,
And leaps.

Transformation

When the end of the world comes,
They won't be sad.
They'll stand there on the shore
In the red of the setting sun, saying,
My, my,
Isn't that beautiful?

About the Author

Liz Kellebrew writes poetry, short fiction, and essays from the Pacific Northwest. She wrote her debut poetry book, *Water Signs* (Unsolicited Press), while riding the ferry between Seattle and Bainbridge Island. Her poems have appeared in public art installations and literary journals such as *About Place, Room*, and *Writers Resist*. She received The Miracle Monocle Award for Innovative Writing, and her fiction has been shortlisted for the Calvino Prize. It also appears in various anthologies and journals, including *The Conium Review, The Coachella Review*, and *Unreal Magazine*. A member of the Academy of American Poets, she holds an MFA in Creative Writing from Goddard College. Learn more at lizkellebrew.com.

About the Press

Unsolicited Press is a small publishing house in Portland, Oregon and is dedicated to producing works of fiction, poetry, and nonfiction from a range of voices, but especially the underserved. The team is comprised of hardworking volunteers that are passionate about literature.

Learn more at www.unsolicitedpress.com.

Find the team on Twitter and Instagram: @unsolicitedp

9 781956 692303